The Science of Soldiers

by Lucia Raatma

Content Consultant
Raymond L. Puffer, PhD
Historian, Ret.,
Edwards Air Force Base
History Office

COMPASS POINT BOOKS
a capstone imprint

Compass Point Books
1710 Roe Crest Drive
North Mankato, MN 56003

Editor: Angie Kaelberer
Designers: Tracy Davies McCabe and Heidi Thompson
Media Researcher: Svetlana Zhurkin
Library Consultant: Kathleen Baxter
Production Specialist: Danielle Ceminsky

Library of Congress Cataloging-in-Publication Data
Raatma, Lucia.
  The science of soldiers / by Lucia Raatma.
      p. cm. — (Science of war)
  "Compass Point Books."
  Includes bibliographical references and index.
  Summary: "Describes the science concepts behind military tactics."—Provided
by publisher.
  Audience: Grades 4 to 6.
  ISBN 978-0-7565-4460-7 (library binding) — ISBN 978-0-7565-4526-0 (paperback)
  1. Soldiers—United States—Juvenile literature. 2. United States—Armed Forces—
Equipment and supplies—Juvenile literature. 3. Military art and science—United
States—Juvenile literature. I. Title. II. Series.
  UA25.D416 2012
  355.4'2—dc23   2011035878

Image Credits:
AP Photo: PRNewsFoto/Raytheon Company, 43, The Montana Standard/Lisa Kunkel, 33; Defense
Imagery, 19; Library of Congress, 18; Newscom: HO Market Wire Photos, 41; Shutterstock:
Daniiel, back cover (top), ella1977, back cover (bottom); U.S. Air Force: A1C Daniel DeCook, 14,
Airman 1st Class Corey Hook, 13 (top), Master Sgt. Scott Thompson, 38, Senior Airman Brian J.
Ellis, 24, Senior Airman Josie Walck, 34, Senior Airman Renae Kleckner, 36, Staff Sgt. Angela
Ruiz, 21, Staff Sgt. Daylena Gonzalez, 13 (bottom), Tech. Sgt. Efren Lopez, 20; U.S. Army: Cpl.
Robert Thaler, 4, Sgt. 1st Class Rob Barker, 32, Sgt. Angelica Golindano, 6, Sgt. Joseph Watson,
1, 5, Spc. Kristina Gupton, 28, Spc. Michael Vanpool, 40, Spec. Olanrewaju Akinwunmi, 29, Staff
Sgt. Edward Daileg, 10, Staff Sgt. James Selesnick, 25, Staff Sgt. Russell Lee Klika, 11, Staff Sgt.
Ryan C. Matson, 26, Timothy L. Hale, 9; U.S. Marine Corps: 2nd Lieutenant Michael Bell, 22, Cpl.
Albert F. Hunt, 27, Cpl. Brian J. Slaght, 31, Cpl. Spencer M. Murphy, 8, Lance Cpl. David Nygren,
15, Lance Cpl. Matthew Hutchison, cover, Sgt. Benjamin R. Reynolds, 23; U.S. Navy: Mass
Communication Specialist (SCW/AW) Class Mark A. Rankin, 16, Mass Communication Specialist
1st Class David P. Coleman, 7; USDA, 17

Visit Compass Point Books on the Internet at *www.capstonepub.com*
Printed in the United States of America in Eau Claire, Wisconsin.
092013   007724R

Contents

Science and Soldiers

1

It is a brutally hot day in Afghanistan. A soldier is sweating underneath his thick vest and camouflage helmet. His combat boots are heavy, but they offer his feet support in the rough terrain.

He and the other soldiers he was traveling with were ambushed. Everyone scattered. He thinks most of his unit made their way out of town and into the hills. But now he's trapped.

The soldier knows there are enemies lying in wait just around the next wall. He's heard the machine gun fire, but he isn't sure if they know his position. He's taken cover behind the rubble of a building, trying to decide what to do next.

Slowly he extends his rifle around one corner of the building. A video camera is built into the rifle's sight. It focuses on the enemy, zooms in, and gathers images for the soldier. These images appear on a display in the soldier's helmet.

The soldier takes a deep breath and thinks for a moment. He considers how much ammunition he has, and he wonders how far away the rest of his unit is.

Next he presses a switch on his rifle, and a laser range finder turns on. It measures the distance to his enemy. The range finder relays this information to a data chip inside the rifle's high-explosive shell. He sets the round to explode just above the enemies' heads. He squeezes the trigger. Shrapnel rains down on the enemy group. Then there is silence.

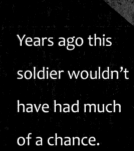

The soldier knows he has given himself a window of opportunity. He races down the street and toward the hills, hoping he'll regroup with the others from his unit.

Years ago this soldier wouldn't have had much of a chance. But technology allowed him to watch his enemy without putting himself in harm's way. Silent and unseen, he was able to assess the situation and figure out a plan.

SCIENCE saved this soldier.

Years ago this soldier wouldn't have had much of a chance.

Not everyone is able to be a soldier. It takes a certain kind of man or woman to put on a uniform and face danger. For this reason soldiers are carefully screened and thoroughly trained before they go on active duty.

The main branches of the U.S. military are the Army, Navy, Air Force, Marines, and Coast Guard. All of these branches provide critical services in defending the nation. The members of these groups often work together on important missions.

To be combat ready, soldiers have to be physically fit, which involves physiology. They may have to endure scorching days or frigid nights. They might climb mountains, wade through waist-deep water, and carry heavy gear for miles.

When men and women join the military, they go through intensive training periods, sometimes called boot camp. They do exercises and drills every day to hone their physical condition. They work on cardiovascular fitness, which targets their heart rate. Training includes running, biking, and swimming. Soldiers also learn to hike for miles while wearing heavy backpacks.

New Types of Training

In recent years Army training has evolved to accommodate the kinds of conditions soldiers might experience in Afghanistan, Iraq, and other

Obstacle course

When men and women join the military, they go through intensive training periods.

Weight training builds strength and endurance.

countries. Therefore miles-long runs have been replaced by sprints in some training programs.

Soldiers work on strength and endurance. They lift weights and use resistance training to increase their muscle strength. They may test themselves by running obstacle courses, including climbing walls, jumping over bodies of water, and crawling through tunnels. Soldiers also need to be flexible. They stretch their muscles after exercise so they remain limber. Being flexible can help a soldier climb a mountain faster or parachute more effectively from a plane.

The Physiology of AEROBIC FITNESS

Most people know that aerobic exercise is good for the heart, but there is more to it. Aerobic activity uses oxygen to provide energy for all the body's muscles. Soldiers who train aerobically experience the following:

- More air moves through the lungs

- Oxygen moves from the lungs and into the bloodstream.

- As the heart pumps faster, more oxygen-rich blood is delivered to the muscles.

- The blood vessels change size to move blood away from inactive muscles and toward active ones.

Maintaining a Healthy Weight

Most military groups require soldiers to meet specific body composition standards. This means they have a healthy weight based on their height. Body mass index (BMI) is a number that calculates body fat, based on height and weight. In general, a normal BMI is between 18.5 and 24.9, but some professional athletes can be healthy and have a higher BMI. Most military groups require that soldiers have a BMI of 27.5 or lower. It is important that they don't have extra pounds to slow them down when they are in combat. Also, extra weight can lead to a higher risk of injury or disease.

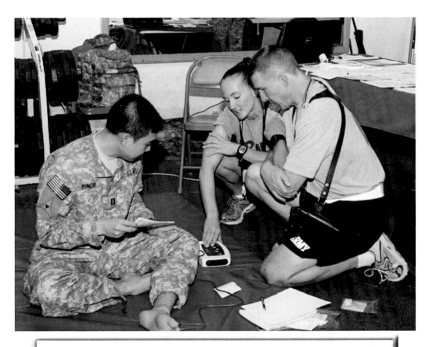

Military members use handheld monitors to measure body fat.

M4 carbine rifle

Specialized Training

After basic training many soldiers go through other preparation for specific areas of the military. Soldiers may train to be pilots, military police officers, or intelligence officers.

Pilots learn about airplanes and helicopters and how to fly them. Military police officers serve as law enforcement within military units. Intelligence officers learn about military strategy and tactics. These soldiers need intelligence and good decision-making abilities to do their jobs well. Their training takes place in both the classroom and the field.

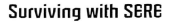

Surviving with SERE

SERE stands for survival, evasion, resistance, and escape. The idea for establishing this military training course began during the Vietnam War (1959-1975), when more than 700 American soldiers were captured and held as prisoners of war in Vietnam. These soldiers endured horrible conditions and torture, which left many of the survivors permanently scarred, both physically and emotionally. Army officials believed that if soldiers were taught to prepare for the treatment they could receive as POWS, as well as escape techniques, they would be much more likely to survive and return home with fewer problems.

Army First Lieutenant Nick Rowe was a POW in Vietnam from 1963 until he managed to escape his captors in 1968. In 1981 the Army asked Rowe to develop and lead its new SERE course. There are three levels of SERE training: A, B, and C. Level C is the most intensive training and is commonly referred to as SERE school. It takes place at the JFK Special Warfare Center at Fort Bragg, North Carolina.

During the three weeks of training, SERE candidates are taught survival techniques and how to avoid enemy troops. They also learn how to resist physical and mental torture if captured, and how to successfully escape. Candidates are deprived both of sleep and food. They eat worms, snakes, and whatever else they can catch. They are

SERE water survival training

chased through the wilderness and then captured and taken to a mock POW camp. There they are subject to physical and mental torture techniques.

Soldiers who successfully complete SERE training generally don't talk about it. However, Chief Warrant Officer Mike Durant said his SERE training helped him survive 10 days of captivity when his Black Hawk helicopter was shot down in Mogadishu, Somalia, in 1993.

Soldiers have to navigate through wilderness.

Training to be a RANGER

Army Ranger School is one of the toughest training programs a soldier can experience. The purpose of this six-week training is to prepare soldiers to lead dangerous and difficult missions. Each day soldiers train for as much as 20 hours and sleep for less than four. They carry between 65 and 90 pounds (30 and 41 kilograms) of gear and hike more than 200 miles (322 kilometers) during the training. Some aspects of the course include:

- Fitness tests of sit-ups, push-ups, and chin-ups

- 5-mile (8-km) runs

- 3-mile (5-km) run in difficult terrain

- 12-mile (19-km) march in full gear

- Water survival assessment

- Land navigation tests

- Explosives training

Currently only male soldiers are eligible for Ranger training.

14

Mental Preparation

For many soldiers, combat is physically demanding. But it can also take its toll psychologically. For this reason many branches of the military offer psychological training and counseling to soldiers.

The U.S. Army has a program called Comprehensive Soldier Fitness. Soldiers who are having psychological problems can take an online self-assessment of their mental health. Depending on their scores, they can then take computer-based courses that teach problem-solving skills and other coping tools. Research is showing that this program is particularly helpful for young soldiers who may lack some of the life experiences more mature soldiers already have.

FITNESS

The Marines have incorporated a yearly fitness test that mimics combat conditions. It includes lifting 30-pound (14-kg) ammunition cans above their heads for a set time and carrying a "wounded" Marine through a 300-yard (274-meter) obstacle course.

3 What Soldiers Eat

Soldiers in active jobs need to eat about 4,500 calories per day.

Nutrition plays a key role in soldiers' fitness levels. They rely on healthy foods to keep them strong.

Most soldiers eat a balanced diet rich in protein, such as lean meat, fish, eggs, beans, and dairy products. They also eat a variety of fruits and vegetables, which are loaded with vitamins and minerals.

Water is also hugely important to soldiers. They know staying hydrated is vital for their everyday health. But water can also save their lives if they are stranded in a hot desert or jungle. Most human bodies are approximately 60 percent water, so it is crucial that soldiers drink enough water to keep their bodies functioning properly.

Good Nutrition

Soldiers need to eat well to maintain a healthy weight. Soldiers who have active jobs such as patrolling need to eat about 4,500 to 5,000 calories each day. Soldiers with desk jobs need 1,800 to 2,500 calories per day.

In 2011 the U.S. Department of Agriculture replaced the standard food pyramid with MyPlate. The plate shows people how each meal should look, with fruits and vegetables taking up half the plate. The rest is made of lean protein and whole grains. Healthy soldiers eat a diet that closely follows the plate.

In 2011 the U.S. Department of Agriculture replaced the standard food pyramid with the food plate.

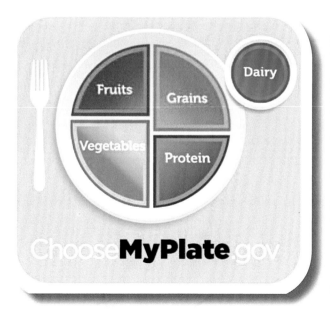

ChooseMyPlate.gov

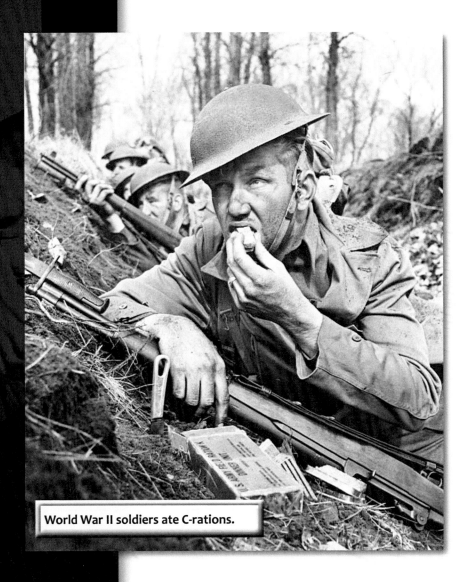

World War II soldiers ate C-rations.

Eating on the Go

On base or in camp, soldiers have cooks who prepare and serve meals in mess halls. But what happens when soldiers are out in the field?

During World War II (1939–1945), most soldiers had to rely on C-rations when they were in the field. C-ration is short for Ration, Combat, Individual. The food was kept fresh by being canned in tins. Soldiers opened the tin with a key attached to the base of each can. A typical meal was meat and vegetable stew. C-rations were famous for being filling but not very tasty.

Canned stew, fruit cocktail, and crackers were part of a typical C-ration meal.

MRE retort pouch

During the Vietnam War soldiers were offered MCIs, which stands for Meal, Combat, Individual. Each meal included meat, fruit, and bread or dessert. The meals were packed in cardboard cartons, which each contained a big can that held the meat entrée and smaller cans of dessert, bread, and fruit. Though the packaging was a little different, soldiers complained that the contents tasted as bad as C-rations.

In the early 1980s, MREs were developed. MRE stands for Meal, Ready to Eat. The meals are preserved in flexible packages, called retort pouches, made of plastic and foil. The raw or partially cooked meals are sealed into the retort pouches. Machines heat the food to 240 to 250 degrees Fahrenheit (115 to 121 degrees Celsius) for several minutes, much like a pressure cooker does. This process prevents the food from spoiling.

Each MRE usually has an entrée such as spaghetti, chicken, or stew, a side dish, bread with peanut butter or cheese spread, a beverage, and

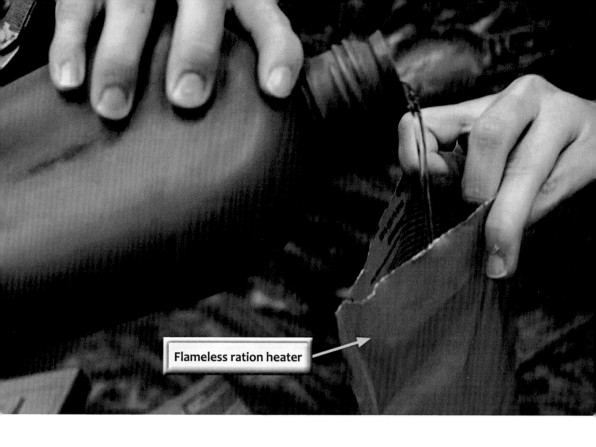

Flameless ration heater

a dessert. An MRE also comes with a flameless heater, so the food can be warmed up before being eaten. Most soldiers agree that the MRE is a vast improvement over the C-ration.

Heating up the MRE involves science. The heaters contain a mixture of powdered sodium, magnesium, and iron. When water is added to the heater, the powdered elements react with the water to instantly form hydrogen gas and heat. The heat lasts long enough to heat the entrée, side dishes, and beverages.

MRE

MREs are tough! They are made to withstand parachute drops of 1,250 feet (380 m).

What Soldiers
Wear and Carry

Camouflage paint and clothing help soldiers blend into the surroundings.

Like chameleons that change color to match their surroundings, soldiers wear camouflage clothing that helps hide them from the enemy.

Camouflage involves the science of how people see color and pattern. Military camouflage consists of several patches of similar colors. People tend to see patches of similar colors as one object, rather than several. In this way the camouflage hides the outline of a soldier's body as it blends with its surroundings. Camouflage might be made of browns and tans for the desert, tans and greens for the jungle, and whites and grays for colder climates. Often a soldier's helmet has the same camouflage.

Kevlar Protection

Camouflage is not the only clothing that helps protect a soldier. Many soldiers wear bullet-resistant vests and helmets made of Kevlar.

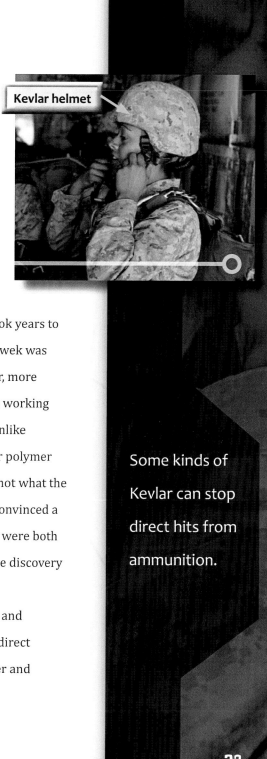

Kevlar helmet

Kevlar is an incredibly strong plastic that holds up in water, is fire resistant, and won't melt. The technology behind Kevlar has helped save thousands of lives.

Manufactured by DuPont, Kevlar took years to develop. In 1965 chemist Stephanie Klowek was trying to develop a material for stronger, more lightweight tires. The polymers she was working with formed liquid crystal, which was unlike other polymers of that time. Initially her polymer solution was thrown away, since it was not what the team was trying to create. But Klowek convinced a technician to test the material, and they were both amazed by how strong the fiber was. The discovery led to the development of Kevlar.

Kevlar is used in tires, gloves, vests, and helmets. Some kinds of Kevlar can stop direct hits from ammunition such as .30-caliber and 9 millimeter bullets.

Some kinds of Kevlar can stop direct hits from ammunition.

Body Armor

Soldiers also wear bulletproof body armor, which is made of ceramic plates lined with Kevlar. One well-used piece of body armor is the outer tactical vest, which also protects the neck and shoulders.

Although body armor is great for protecting soldiers' chests and shoulders, many injuries are to arms and legs. To fight this problem, scientists are working on liquid body armor. The armor would be light and flexible enough to cover a soldier's whole body. Liquid body armor is made of a thick fluid that is poured between layers of Kevlar. The liquid is a mixture of the gaseous materials ethylene and

> Although body armor is great for protecting soldiers' chests and shoulders, many injuries are to arms and legs.

Body armor plate

polyethylene glycol and the compound silica. If the liquid is stirred slowly, the silica moves out of the way, and an object can penetrate it. But if something enters it quickly, the silica seizes up, binds together, and goes rigid. The idea is that the liquid armor could stop a fast-moving bullet in an instant.

Advanced combat helmet

Tracking Helmet

While body armor and Kevlar protect soldiers from bullets, a new kind of helmet may do even more. It uses electrical engineering and acoustics to warn soldiers that there is gunfire close by. The helmet is equipped with four microphones that pick up two types of sound waves—a shock wave from the bullet as it travels and a sound wave from the gun blast. The waves help track the shooter's location, the type of weapon, and the caliber of the bullet. This information is then displayed on a Personal Digital Assistant (PDA) carried by the soldier.

Keeping Comfortable

Staying warm or staying cool is a constant problem for soldiers. One way to deal with this is to wear the right clothing. Soldiers in both warm and cool climates wear undergarments made of wicking fabrics. The fabrics pull moisture from the body, just as a candle pulls wax up the wick to a flame. Wicking fabrics are made of polyester blends woven in a way that forces moisture into and through the gaps in the weave. Some of the materials are also treated with chemicals that won't allow moisture to soak through.

However, one problem with wicking fabric is that it isn't fire resistant. Soldiers can suffer burns and injuries from explosive devices. In 2006 the U.S. Marine Corps designed Flame Resistant Organizational Gear, called FROG. The clothing

Nomex hood

includes under and outer clothes made of fabric that is both wicking and flame resistant. Army soldiers wear similar clothing.

To protect their hands, soldiers wear gloves made of Nomex, which is heat and flame resistant and will wick away perspiration. Many soldiers cut off the index finger of one glove. This gives their firing fingers more control.

Packing It Up

A soldier's rucksack contains an amazing collection of gear. It holds weapons, food, water, ammunition, clothing, and other supplies. Depending on the mission, rucksacks weigh as much as 80 pounds (36 kg).

Carrying such a heavy pack is a disadvantage for soldiers. It can make them less agile and more vulnerable to attack.

Over the years technology has provided better options. One is MOLLE, which stands for Modular Lightweight Load-carrying Equipment. This rucksack is a system of attaching lightweight packs. The packs attach using nylon webbing. The webbing is sewn onto the MOLLE and the attaching packs. The straps on the packs are woven between the webbing and snapped together. This allows a secure, adjustable fit.

MOLLE has a sturdy plastic frame that can withstand temperatures as low as -40 F (-40 C) and as high as 120 F (49 C). The system accommodates 180 rounds of ammunition, 25 pieces of equipment, a 72-ounce (2-kg) hydration bladder that stores drinking water, and two hand grenades. It also can support 18 additional pouches for other supplies.

MOLLE packs

Night vision goggles

Seeing in the Dark

Soldiers fight battles both day and night, so night vision devices have
proven invaluable. The devices work in two ways. They make images
sharper by collecting tiny bits of light—part of the infrared spectrum that

humans can't see—and magnifying them. They also use thermal imaging. The technology detects infrared rays that are produced as heat. For example, human bodies give off more heat than objects such as buildings or rocks.

Some night vision devices come with an infrared spotlight lens, a compass, and a high-magnification lens. Night vision devices also can be mounted on helmets.

Today's military rifles are equipped with amazing high-tech accessories. Among them are video camera gun sights that allow soldiers to see their target while still remaining protected. The sights also have night-vision capabilities, so soldiers can determine the danger around them even in the dark.

NANO

The Institute for Soldier Nanotechnologies is a research center at the Massachusetts Institute of Technology. It was founded in 2002 with the goal of using nanotechnology—the science of altering atoms and molecules—to improve soldiers' battle gear. For example, a waterproof poncho could be replaced by a nano-thin coating on everything that the soldier wears or carries.

FACE PAINT

Wearing camouflage helps soldiers blend in, but that still leaves their faces exposed. For this reason many soldiers rely on camouflage face paint. It comes in tubes and sticks, and is available in various colors of green, tan, and gray. It's made mainly of wax, so it lasts for a long time. Some types of paint are more waterproof than others.

Soldiers are trained to apply the paint so their faces, ears, and necks become nearly invisible in the field. Most Army units follow a specific pattern that all soldiers learn. The Marines sometimes use a pattern that is specific to their division.

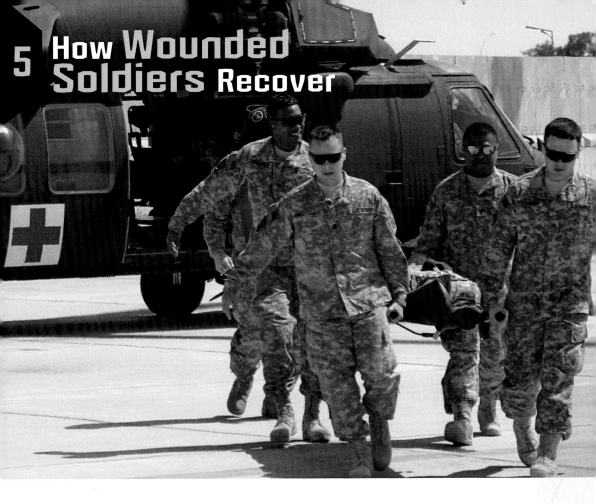

5 How Wounded Soldiers Recover

Many years ago it was all too common for wounded soldiers to die on the battlefield, even from minor injuries. Advances in technology are now helping soldiers get faster, more effective treatment.

Amazing Inventions

One of the greatest concerns for soldiers in combat is loss of blood. Soldiers in Iraq and Afghanistan are using bandages coated with kaolin. Kaolin is derived from clay and acts as a drying agent for wounds. Bandages made with the material can save lives by clotting blood and stopping blood loss in a matter of minutes.

Other bandages use tiny sea creatures as a clotting agent. Chitosan is a biopolymer made from chitin, an element found in the exoskeletons of crab, shrimp, and other crustaceans. Chitosan has a positive ion charge that attracts the negatively charged outer membranes of red blood cells. When the two meet, clotting occurs.

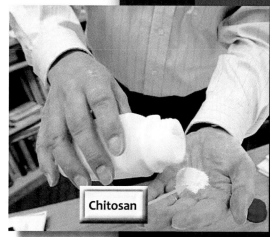

Chitosan

A drug currently in development is also showing great promise. The drug is not yet named, but it would help a wounded soldier's body to shut down until medical treatment can start. Usually an injured soldier goes into shock, a life-threatening condition in which the heart rate and blood pressure shoot up.

During shock, 6 to 7 percent of the person's genes change their expression, removing chemical reactions called acetylations. The new drug would use histone deacetylase (HDAC) inhibitors to prevent acetylation removal and shock symptoms from occurring. The HDAC inhibitor could also slow blood loss and give the soldier precious time before treatment could start.

Military doctors are conducting research on vascular injuries.

Field Medicine

Field medics were once trained only in first aid. Now many of them are fully licensed emergency medical technicians, so they are better prepared to treat a much wider variety of injuries. They know how to evaluate injuries, control bleeding, set broken bones, and open blocked airways.

Some field medics use night-vision technology to better see soldiers' veins and arteries before treatment. The Vascular Viewer uses an infrared light source to see a wounded soldier's veins and arteries. The light source is placed under a wound, and a medic looks through a night-vision monoscope. The infrared light illuminates the soldier's body parts. The Vascular Viewer helps medics insert needles and intravenous lines properly, even in low-light conditions.

Doctors can use handheld ultrasound computers to help diagnose internal injuries or other conditions. Thanks to modern computer technology and the Internet, they can also use handheld PDAs to record and track medical information. A doctor in the field can then send a soldier's medical records to a hospital miles away.

Treating PTSD

Some military injuries aren't easily visible. Soldiers who have been in combat or under attack can suffer from post-traumatic stress disorder. People with PTSD may have flashbacks or nightmares about the traumatic event. They also may have difficulty coping with everyday life.

The Virtual Iraq computer program is used to treat PTSD.

Traditional treatments for PTSD include talk therapy and medications such as antidepressants. They will likely continue to be used in the future. However, the military is also studying alternative therapies that take advantage of advances in technology.

One of the therapies involves virtual reality. The technology can recreate the sights, sounds, smells, and feelings of the traumatic situation in a safe place, such as a doctor's office.

Researchers are also studying cortisol, a hormone people produce in response to stress. They want to know if using medication to increase cortisol levels in people will prevent or reduce the symptoms of PTSD.

Other studies involve mice, whose brains show various mechanisms for adapting or being overwhelmed by stress. Human brains also have similar mechanisms. Scientists hope to use and enhance this ability to help people deal with highly stressful situations.

Bluetooth Prosthetics

Gunfire, land mines, or improvised explosive devices all can cause a soldier to lose an arm or leg. Years ago these soldiers would be fitted with prosthetic limbs that were made of wood, plastic, or metal. Today soldiers still use artificial limbs, but a new generation of prosthetics can help soldiers regain full use of their bodies.

Many cell phones use Bluetooth technology for communication. Bluetooth uses short wavelength radio signals to send data over short distances. Now some prosthetic limbs are using the technology as well. A Bluetooth device is mounted on a soldier's ankle, which allows the artificial leg to coordinate its movement with the other leg. The technology even works for soldiers with two prosthetic limbs.

Soldiers use GPS equipment to find their location and locate enemy targets.

Hundreds of years ago, soldiers relied mostly on their weapons and their instincts. Today these things are still important, but technology is playing a greater role all the time.

Navigation

Today many drivers use the global positioning system (GPS) to help them find their way in unfamiliar places. The Department of Defense created the navigation system in the 1970s to help guide missiles.

GPS is composed of 24 satellites that orbit Earth. The satellites circle Earth twice each day and are used to calculate the position of objects on Earth. A GPS receiver locates four or more of the satellites. Then it determines its distance to each one based on how long it takes a radio signal to travel from the receiver to the satellite. When all this information overlaps, the receiver can calculate its location. Soldiers use GPS to determine their positions, as well as the positions of the enemy.

Soldiers need batteries to operate PDAs and other electronic devices.

Communicating from the War Zone

Years ago soldiers could only communicate with family and friends back home by letter. The letters often took weeks to reach their destinations. Today many soldiers use computers and social media websites to communicate with each other and with their families. When they have free time, soldiers update their Facebook pages, upload videos to YouTube, and tweet short messages on their Twitter accounts. The tools allow soldiers to record their experiences and transmit them in real time.

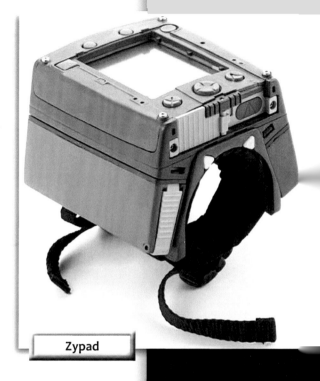

Zypad

Carrying a computer in the field can be impractical for a soldier. But one type of computer fits on a soldier's wrist. The little wrist computer has a flexible screen and is very sturdy, so it can withstand a soldier's normal activities. One version is called the Zypad. It includes GPS, flash drive, WiFi, and Bluetooth. Soldiers also use tablet computers.

On a five-day mission, a soldier uses an average of 88 AA batteries.

All the technology is a great service to soldiers, but keeping it all charged can be problem. Soldiers may not have access to reliable power sources. Batteries can be a solution, but they have a limited amount of power and add extra weight to a soldier's gear. In 2008 the U.S. Department of Energy sponsored a contest for companies to develop a lightweight wearable power system that would run continuously for four days. The winners were systems that combine fuel cells powered by methanol, propane, or hydrogen with rechargeable batteries. Each of the systems weighs less than 9 pounds (4 kg).

Futuristic Advances

Future science and technology may transform soldiers even more. Researchers are working on a tool called an exoskeleton. The mechanical framework would fit over a soldier's body. It would need to be strong but not too heavy. Titanium is one metal being tested. Using electronics or hydraulics, the exoskeleton would improve a soldier's leg and arm movements. It would make the soldier able to easily carry loads weighing as much as 200 pounds (91 kg).

Future science and technology may transform soldiers even more.

The military is testing an exoskeleton, which will give soldiers more strength.

As technology evolves, the daily lives of soldiers will continue to change. They will still need their strength, courage, and instincts, but soldiers will rely more and more on science. It will help them fight longer, be more effective, and stay safer than ever before.

Glossary

acetylation—a chemical reaction in the body caused by introducing the acetyl radical

acoustics—technology that relies on hearing and sound

camouflage—coloring or covering that makes animals, people, and objects look like their surroundings

exoskeleton— a bony or hard covering on the outside of an animal; also a human-made supporting structure worn on the outside of the body

histone deacetylase inhibitors—compounds that can block certain chemical reactions in the body

hydraulics—technology that gets power from liquid forced through pipes or chambers

infrared light—light that produces heat; humans cannot see infrared light

physiology—the study of how the body works

shrapnel—small pieces of metal that are scattered by an exploding shell or bomb

ultrasound—an imaging system that uses sound waves to see inside the human body

vascular—a system of channels that transport fluids, such as veins in the human body

Read More

Adams, Simon. *Eyewitness Soldier.* New York: DK, 2009.

Goldish, Meish. *Army: Civilian to Soldier.* New York: Bearport Publishing, 2011.

Labrecque, Ellen. *Special Forces.* Chicago: Raintree, 2012.

Internet Sites

Use FactHound to find Internet sites related to this book. All of the sites on FactHound have been researched by our staff.

Here's all you do:
Visit *www.facthound.com*
Type in this code: 9780756544607

Read all the books in this series:

Science of Military Vehicles
Science of Soldiers
Science of Weapons

Select Bibliography

Body Armor. 15 Aug. 2011. www.bodyarmornews.com/
bodyarmordevelopments/bodyarmor-recent-developments.htm

Fitness and Nutrition. 15 Aug. 2011. www.goarmy.com/content/goarmy/
soldier-life/fitness-and-nutrition.html

Halberstadt, Hans. *Battle Rattle: The Stuff a Soldier Carries.*
St. Paul: Zenith Press, 2006.

Hendren, John. "Medical Treatment Advances Help Injured Soldiers."
NPR. 10 May 2006. 15 Aug. 2011. www.npr.org/templates/story/story.
php?storyId=5395423

Kevlar Brand Aramid Fiber. 15 Aug. 2011. www2.dupont.com/Kevlar/en_US/

Montgomery, Nancy. "Building the warrior within: Comprehensive Soldier
Fitness program aims to boost soldiers' psychological resiliency." *Stars
and Stripes.* 25 Sept. 2010. 15 Aug. 2011. www.stripes.com/building-the-
warrior-within-comprehensive-soldier-fitness-program-aims-to-boost-
soldiers-psychological-resiliency-1.119529

Nusca, Andrew. "With new drug, scientists fortify injured soldiers to keep
them alive until medical treatment arrives." Smart Plantet. 1 Feb. 2010. 15
Aug. 2011. www.smartplanet.com/business/blog/smart-takes/with-new-
drug-scientists-fortify-injured-soldiers-to-keep-them-alive-until-medical-
treatment-arrives/3760

Soldier Safety: Sniper-Detecting Helmet. 15 Aug. 2011. www.ivanhoe.com/
science/story/2010/04/698a.html

Top 5 Gadgets on the High-Tech Soldier. How Stuff Works. 15 Aug. 2011.
http://science.howstuffworks.com/5-gadgets-high-tech-soldier2.htm

Vizard, Frank, and Phil Scott. *21st Century Soldier: The Weaponry, Gear, and
Technology in the New Century.* New York: Bishop Books, 2002.

Index

About the author

Lucia Raatma has written many books for young
readers. She especially enjoys writing about science,
sports, history, animals, and famous people. She lives
in the Tampa Bay area with her husband and their
two children.